WONDERS!
Our World in Fact and Fiction

ANIMALS AND THEIR YOUNG

Lada Josefa Kratky

 **HAMPTON-BROWN BOOKS**

illustrated with photographs

Hampton-Brown Books
P.O. Box 223220
Carmel, California 93922

Printed in the United States of America
ISBN 1–56334–054–2

91 92 93 94 95 96 97 98 99 00 10 9 8 7 6 5 4 3 2 1

Illustrations: Sharron O'Neil
Photographs: The Image Bank: cover, pp. 1, 12; Animals/Animals: back cover, pp. 4a, 4b,5,
6a, 6b, 6c, 6d, 7a, 7b, 8, 9, 10a, 10b, 10c, 10d, 11a, 11b, 11c, 11d, 11e, 13, 14, 16, 21, 18, 22,
23, 24; Robert Long: p. 15; SuperStock: pp. 17, 20; Grant Heilman Inc; R.S Virdee: p. 19

Have you ever seen a litter of frisky puppies? Cute, aren't they? Animals are small when they're born, but they will all grow up to be just like their parents.

Some animals hatch from eggs. Fish lay their eggs in the water. When the little fish hatch, they already know how to take care of themselves.

Snakes also lay eggs.
Snakes do not need to feed
their young. Little snakes
know how to take care
of themselves.

All birds hatch from eggs.

Birds' eggs can be very different in size. A hummingbird egg (left) seems tiny in comparison with a hen's egg (center). An ostrich egg (right) is enormous.

Mother birds take care of their young. This bird will feed her young until they are old enough to leave the nest and search for their own food.

This drawing shows the parts of an egg.

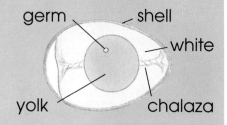

germ   shell
                white
yolk   chalaza

Break an egg on a plate. Can you see all the parts?

The chick develops from the **germ**, a tiny spot on the yolk. The **white** and the **yolk** provide food for the chick while it is inside the egg. The **chalaza** is a kind of cord that keeps the yolk in the middle of the egg. The **shell** protects the chick as it develops.

When chicks hatch, they already know how to scratch for food. The hen protects them and keeps them warm.

These ducklings are looking for food in the water. A mother duck defends her ducklings when other animals come near.

1. The female lays eggs.

2. A tadpole hatches from an egg.

3. Little by little, the tadpole loses its tail, and its legs appear.

4. The tadpole becomes a frog.

Some animals that hatch from eggs go through a number of changes before they become adults.

For example, **tadpoles**, or newly hatched frogs, don't look anything like adult frogs. Little by little, tadpoles change and become frogs.

Another animal that goes through great changes after hatching is the butterfly.

FROM EGG TO BUTTERFLY

1. Butterflies lay eggs.

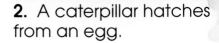

2. A caterpillar hatches from an egg.

3. The caterpillar spins itself a **cocoon**.

4. A butterfly comes out of the cocoon.

Not all animals hatch from eggs. Some grow inside their mother's body before being born. Among these animals are the **mammals**. Mammals are born live.

Most mammals live on land, but there are some that live in the water.

Whales are the world's largest mammals. A newborn whale can be the size of a school bus!

Some mammals give birth to one baby at a time.

THAT'S A
FACT!

An armadillo always gives birth to 4 babies. There may be 4 males or 4 females, but never both males and females in the same litter.

Others give birth to several babies at a time.

17

Mammal mothers have to teach their young to find food. This mother bear is teaching her cub to fish.

This lioness is teaching her cub to hunt.

This table shows the speed of a few animals that depend on speed in order to escape their predators.

Animal	Time It Takes to Run 25 Meters
Gazelle	1 second
Hare	2 seconds
Ostrich	1 second

Go to the playground with a few of your classmates. Ask your teacher to use a stopwatch to measure how long it takes each of you to run 25 meters. Write down the results. Compare them with the animals on the chart. Who is fastest? Is anyone faster than a gazelle or an ostrich?

Many mammals depend on their speed to survive.

The mothers of these mammals teach their young to recognize signs of danger, such as suspicious scents and noises. When they sense danger, they run to escape.

Wolf cubs learn while they play. These cubs are having fun, but they are also learning skills that will make them good hunters when they grow up. Wolves depend on their hunting skills in order to survive.

As you have seen, a mammal's "childhood" is a very important time. That is when it learns everything it needs to know to survive as an adult.

All animals start out as
babies. That's how you
started out, too.